# Fearless
## in the
# Light

*Staying Calm in Today's Anxious World*

By
**Max Girgenti**

**Edizioni Dunamis**

Published by Edizioni Dunamis
Via Monte Pastello 6/b
San Giovanni Lupatoto,
Verona 37057 Italy

*A Honey from the Rock series*

ISBN: 9788864230603

Emphasis in Scripture shown by italics is the author's.

Unless otherwise identified, Scripture quotations are from the Holy Bible, *New Living Translation (NLT).* (2007). Tyndale.

Scripture quotations identified *NKJ* are from the *New King James Version (NKJV).* (1982). Thomas Nelson.

Scripture quotations identified *AMP* are from the *Amplified Version (AMP).* (1987). Zondervan.

Scripture quotations identified *Expanded Bible* are from the *Expanded Bible (Expanded Bible).* (2011). Thomas Nelson.

Edizioni Dunamis
Via Monte Pastello, 6/b - S. Giovanni Lupatoto (VR)

# Dedication

*This book is dedicated to my lovely wife Connie, my companion and partner in life for 36 spectacular years.*

*She is a precious gift from God; her help and support are invaluable. Her constant encouragement has kept me going, and her intimate and uncompromising walk with God is a great inspiration to me and to all who know her.*

*Life has been a wonderful adventure with you, honey, and I look forward to serving God together with you for many more exciting decades. I love you with all my heart!*

*This book is also dedicated to our three gorgeous princesses: Laura, Deborah and Sarah.*

*Girls, thank you for sticking with dad through the many challenges of being pastor's daughters. Your love for God and your achievements in life are also an inspiration to me. You are lights shining bright in my life, and I love you with all my heart!*

# *Contents*

Preface ............................................................. 6

Introduction ..................................................... 7

1. Light ............................................................. 9

2. More Light ................................................... 14

3. Salvation ..................................................... 21

4. Fortress ...................................................... 27

5. Fear ........................................................... 33

6. Enemies and Adversaries .............................. 40

7. Wars and Armies ........................................ 54

8. Heavy Lifting ............................................. 63

9. Which Temple? ........................................... 68

10. The Secret ................................................ 75

Appendix: Pantophobia no more ....................... 87

The Most Important Decision in Life ................. 88

# *Preface*

A *Honey from the Rock* book:

> **Deuteronomy 32:13 "He made him ride in the heights of the earth, That he might eat the produce of the fields; He made him draw honey from the rock, And oil from the flinty rock."**

The *Honey from the Rock* book series mission:

Quick meditations, packed with useful information and filled with practical advice.

Easily read in one sitting, *Honey from the Rock* is a quick boost to charge up your spiritual walk with God.

Doctrinally accurate, with scholarly cross-references, *Honey from the Rock* will enrich your knowledge of the Word of God.

Carry *Honey from the Rock* with you in your smartphone, tablet, PC and print version - whichever you prefer.

# *Introduction*

I would like to share with you the inspiration for this book.

On March 22, 2017, I was riding the subway in the great city of London, in transit from Gatwick to Heathrow airport. Suddenly, the conductor stopped the train and a voice over a loudspeaker announced that we had stopped because some kind of an "incident" had occurred. He did not explain what the "incident" was.

As I usually do, when I find myself in uncertain circumstances, I turned on my tablet, opened my Bible, and turned my thoughts to the Word of God. This time, I chose to meditate on the twenty-seventh Psalm.

Approximately twenty minutes later the train started moving again, and I arrived at my hotel. When I entered the lobby, and glanced at the television screens, I realized that the train had been stopped because a terrorist attack had occurred near the Palace of Westminster.

When I returned home, my oldest daughter Laura asked me about the incident. I told her what happened and what I did. In talking to her I said, "...naturally, I opened my Bible, like most Christians do when facing uncertain or difficult situations". She said to me that it was her experience that "most" Christians she knew did not "naturally" gravitate to Scripture when facing the unknown. Laura then proceeded to suggest that maybe I should do some teaching on this subject.

This got me thinking about how we react to uncertain events. In our western culture, fear and anxiety levels seem to be at an all-time high.[1] I prayed about it and decided to follow Laura's suggestion. I taught on this subject in church, and the reaction from the congregation was extremely positive.

This is how this book was born.

This book is *not* about the tragic, complex topic of terrorism. It's not even about literal armies and wars between nations. It took me many years to learn this lesson: I simply cannot control what other people do. This book is about controlling the only thing I can control: *me*. It's about how I confront challenges in my personal life. In virtually every situation I face, I can choose my thoughts and what I say, I can control my feelings, and I can choose how I react to people around me.

In times of personal trouble, is there someone I can go to in order to find some answers? How can I deal with the difficult people I encounter? How do I stay calm in a world that is filled with anxiety?

We will try to answer these questions by meditating on the twenty-seventh Psalm. In this powerful passage of Scripture, King David is dealing with his inner fears and with a myriad of external difficulties. In it, he reveals some important secrets to overcoming the problems that we face in life. We will study these vital secrets in as much detail as possible.

Let's get started.

---

1) Anxiety and Depression Association of America: Panic disorder, 6 million; Social anxiety disorder, 15 million; specific phobias, 19 million. "Facts and Statistics." https://www.adaa.org/about-adaa/press-room/facts-statistics (accessed June 22, 2017).

# Chapter 1
# Light

## Let there be light

The first verse of Psalm 27 states:

**Psalms 27:1 The Lord is my light and my salvation—so why should I be afraid? The Lord is my fortress, protecting me from danger, so why should I tremble?**

The Lord is my light. *The Lord is my light.* This is a wonderful phrase to meditate while going through difficult times. Reciting this Psalm will calm our minds, restore peace to our hearts and strengthen our faith. It did for David, and it will do the same for us.

The Lord is my *light.* Since the Lord is light, it would be good for us to see what the Bible says about light.

Let's start by looking at John's first epistle:

**1 John 1:5 This is the message we heard from Jesus and now declare to you: God is light, and there is no darkness in him at all.**

The apostle John confirms the important truth that God is light. The Bible makes this clear right from the start.

The Book of Genesis reveals to us that in the beginning God created the heavens and the earth.[2] God created everything, including light. Now notice this important detail in the creation story:

---

2) Genesis 1:1 In the beginning God created the heavens and the earth.

**Genesis 1:2 The earth was formless and empty, and darkness covered the deep waters. And the Spirit of God was hovering over the surface of the waters.**

The earth was formless, empty and was covered with darkness: it seems like things were rather chaotic. Amid this chaos, God spoke and commanded:

**Genesis 1:3 Then God said, "Let there be light," and there was light.**

God said "light" and light was. There was darkness, and the very first thing God said is "light be".

Then God saw the light, and He saw that it was good:

**Genesis 1:4 And God saw that the light was good. Then he separated the light from the darkness.**

The author of the book of Genesis narrates that before there was ever a man, a church, or a church choir on earth to sing His praises, God looked at what He had just done and saw that it was good. Right from the start, the Bible introduces us to a God who does good things and who has no problem at all expressing Himself in positive terms. God is complete in Himself and He does not *need* anyone to worship Him. He does not have a fragile ego that needs constant affirmation with our adoration. God does not demand worship: Jesus said that He is looking for *worshipers*.[3] He is looking for people who want to spend time with Him. Worship is not for God's benefit, it's for our benefit: it lifts our hearts up to commune

---

3) John 4:23 But the hour is coming, and now is, when the true worshipers will worship the Father in spirit and truth; for the Father is seeking such to worship Him. (NKJV)

with an infinite God, and it lifts our minds to His higher way of thinking. Being in His presence transforms us and makes us better human beings.

Everything we just discussed happened on day one of creation. Three days later, on day four, God set in motion the sun, moon and stars:

**Genesis 1:14-18 Then God said, "Let lights appear in the sky to separate the day from the night. Let them be signs to mark the seasons, days, and years. ¹⁵ Let these lights in the sky shine down on the earth." And that is what happened. ¹⁶ God made two great lights—the larger one to govern the day, and the smaller one to govern the night. He also made the stars. ¹⁷ God set these lights in the sky to light the earth, ¹⁸ to govern the day and night, and to separate the light from the darkness. And God saw that it was good. ¹⁹ And evening passed and morning came, marking the fourth day.**

Clearly, the larger light is the sun and the lesser light is the moon. Once more God sees that this is good (v.18). Keep in mind that as we already mentioned, this happened on the fourth day.

By now you may be asking, what does all this have to do with the fact that God is light? Well, we have seen that on day *one* God created light, and on day *four* He created the sun, moon and stars. In other words, the sun did not begin to shine, as it does today, until the fourth day. The obvious question then is as follows: what kind of light lit up the earth during the first three days? It was the light of God; it was God Himself.

I wish I had been there to see this extraordinary phenomenon, don't you? The good news is that what happened in the first four days of creation is not a one-time event. The last book in the Bible reveals to us that it will happen again in the future, in the new heavens and the new earth:

**Revelation 21:23 And the city has no need of sun or moon, for the glory of God illuminates the city, and the Lamb is its light.**

The heavenly Jerusalem will not need the sun or moon, or for that matter any other kind of natural light source, because God Himself will light everything up. I am really looking forward to personally experiencing this spectacular event!

In the book of Genesis, we saw how the earth was without form, empty and covered in darkness. Amid all the darkness and chaos, God decreed light into existence. This means that in times of darkness, confusion and chaos, I can still find my way around life because God is my light. He shines His light in my times of darkness, He illumines my path and gives me direction. He brings order out of chaos, making a way where there is no way. Since *He* is my light, even if it doesn't look like it, I am blessed just because He says I am blessed.[4] I can obey Him and serve Him because He is working in me, giving me the desire and the power to carry out His will.[5] He is my glory and He supplies everything I need according to His riches in *glory*.[6] Christ is complete,

---

4) Ephesians 1:3 Blessed be the God and Father of our Lord Jesus Christ, who has blessed us with every spiritual blessing in the heavenly places in Christ (NKJV).
5) Philippians 2:13 For God is working in you, giving you the desire and the power to do what pleases him.
6) Philippians 4:19 For God is working in you, giving you the desire and the power to do what pleases him.

and I am complete in Him.[7] All the wonderful truths we just mentioned are realities in my life not because it looks like I have it all together (I don't), not even because I feel good all the time (I don't): they are real because God declared them concerning me in His Word!

When believed, these powerful Bible truths have the power to transform our lives.

**The Lord is my light!**

---

7) Colossians 2:9-10 9 For in Him dwells all the fullness of the Godhead bodily; 10 and you are complete in Him, who is the head of all principality and power. (NKJV).

# Chapter 2
# *More Light*

## *Other sources of light*

In the last chapter, we saw that God is light. The Bible teaches us that there are other sources of light. Let's look at some of them.

Let's re-read a verse we just looked at in the last chapter:

**Revelation 21:23 And the city has no need of sun or moon, for the glory of God illuminates the city, and the Lamb is its light.**

*The Lamb is light.* This verse tells us that the Lamb, or Jesus, is the light of God's city.

Jesus Himself said:

**John 8:12 …"I am the light of the world. If you follow me, you won't have to walk in darkness, because you will have the light that leads to life."**

So, not only is God light, but Jesus also is light.

We can take this a step further. Since Jesus is the Word,[8] then we can accurately say that the Word of God is light. Which is exactly what King David wrote in Psalm 119:

**Psalms 119:105 Your word is a lamp to guide my feet and a light for my path.**

---

8) John 1:1 In the beginning was the Word, and the Word was with God, and the Word was God. (NKJV).

This verse has a real practical application. When I am in a dark room, I can't see, I don't know where I am going and I may trip over something. As soon as I turn on the light, I see what is around me and I can walk around freely without bumping into anything. Light illuminates spiritually as well as physically. The Word of God lights my path in life: He shows me what to say, what to do, where to go and how to act.[9]

So, God is light, Jesus is light and the Word is light. But there is more.

The apostle Paul makes it clear that it is the Holy Spirit who gives us revelation. Here is what he wrote in the book of Corinthians:

**1 Corinthians 2:9 That is what the Scriptures mean when they say, "No eye has seen, no ear has heard, and no mind has imagined what God has prepared for those who love him."**

God has prepared wonderful things for everyone who loves Him. How exactly can we know what He has prepared for us? The next verse explains it to us:

**1 Corinthians 2:10 But it was to us that God revealed these things by his Spirit. For his Spirit searches out everything and shows us God's deep secrets.**

God reveals them to us *by His Spirit*. This means that the Holy Spirit brings light also. After all, the term *revelation* covers the ideas of "making obscure things clear, bringing

---

9) John 8:28-29 So Jesus said, "...I do nothing on my own but say only what the Father taught me. 29 And the one who sent me is with me—he has not deserted me. For I always do what pleases him."

hidden things to light, causing the persons addressed to see."[10] Therefore, when the Holy Spirit reveals things to us, He is shedding light in our hearts and minds.

Read again verse 9 above. Note that God "has prepared" these things. He will not prepare them someday in the future; He has already prepared them. They are already there. An important part of living by faith is realizing that God has already prepared wonderful things for us. Even though we may not see them, God has already given us all things.[11]

Sometimes we have a hard time grasping the concept of believing for things that we cannot see. Some object, "How can I say that I already have something which I cannot see?" The common wisdom of the world states, "first I'll see it, then I'll believe it". Which, by the way, is exactly what Thomas said.[12] Jesus did not exactly endorse this way of seeing things. In marked contrast to this, faith says the exact opposite: "first I'll believe it, then I'll see it." Here is the verse to prove it:

**Mark 11:24 I tell you, you can pray for anything, and if you believe that you've received it, it will be yours.**

First we believe, then we receive. *First we believe, then we see.* In other words, we must be convinced we already have what we are asking before we see it.

---

10) Packer, J. I. (1996). Revelation. In D. R. W. Wood, I. H. Marshall, A. R. Millard, & D. J. Wiseman (Eds.), New Bible dictionary (3rd ed., p. 1014). Leicester, England; Downers Grove, IL: InterVarsity Press.

11) 1 Corinthians 3:21-22 21 Therefore let no one boast in men. For all things are yours: 22 whether Paul or Apollos or Cephas, or the world or life or death, or things present or things to come—all are yours. (NKJV).
Romans 8:32 Since he did not spare even his own Son but gave him up for us all, won't he also give us everything else?

12) John 20:25 "I won't believe it unless I see the nail wounds in his hands, put my fingers into them, and place my hand into the wound in his side."

Actually, we experience this phenomenon often in our everyday life. There are many things we are convinced of having, without ever having seen them. For example, someone jokingly said that people generally believe they have a brain, yet most people have never actually seen it! On a more serious note, we believe that electrons exist, but we have never actually seen them. We can infer their presence, but we can't see them directly.[13] One more practical example pertinent to light: I am sure that one time you may have walked into a totally dark room, where you could not see anything at all. Then you turned on the light and, voilà, you saw all kinds of things. Depending on the room, you may have been surrounded by chairs, desks, and all other kinds of furniture. Now, were all those things already there even when you did not see them? Definitely yes! Did all those things materialize in the room when you turned on the light? Absolutely not! Every piece of furniture was already there, but you were not able to see any of it because it was pitch-dark. But the instant you turned on the light, you were able to clearly see all the things that *were already there.*

The same is true spiritually speaking. God has already prepared many wonderful things for us: they are already there, just like the furniture in the dark room. This is precisely why the apostle Paul prayed that we would have the spirit of wisdom and revelation in the knowledge of Christ:

**Ephesians 1:17 asking God, the glorious Father of our Lord Jesus Christ, to give you spiritual wisdom and insight so that you might grow in your knowledge of God.**

---

13) Physics. "Why can't an electron be observed?" Physics.stackexchange.com. https://physics.stackexchange.com/questions/237350/why-cant-an-electron-be-observed (accessed February 18, 2016).

Paul goes on to explain that when we pray in this fashion, our eyes are *enlightened*, and we come to know many wonderful things that God has prepared for us:

**Ephesians 1:18 I pray that your hearts will be flooded with light so that you can understand the confident hope he has given to those he called—his holy people who are his rich and glorious inheritance.**

When our hearts are flooded with light, we can begin to understand all the many things that God has deposited in us and prepared for us in Christ. Perhaps, when we pray, we should stop asking God for things that the Bible says He has already given us. It may be better for us to pray that God would enlighten us as to what He has already given us, and then simply thank Him for that.

The Lord is my light, indeed!

So, God is light, Jesus is light, the Word is light and the Holy Spirit brings light. One more thought on light - and this one may be quite surprising.

In one of His most famous teachings, the Sermon on the Mount, Jesus said this:

**Matthew 5:14 "You are the light of the world—like a city on a hilltop that cannot be hidden.**

You are the light of the world. Surprise: *you are also light!*

Jesus proceeded to tell us that we must let our light shine:

**Matthew 5:16 In the same way, let your good deeds shine out for all to see, so that everyone will praise your heavenly Father.**

Similarly, Paul not only confirms that we *are* indeed light, but he also exhorts us to walk as children of light:

**Ephesians 5:8 For you were once darkness, but now you are light in the Lord. Walk as children of light (NKJ)**

We don't force our light to shine, we simply let it shine. When we walk as children of light, when we behave like Christians, then our light shines.

So, God is light, Jesus is light, the Word is light, the Holy Spirit brings light and, surprisingly, we are also light.

Today, in many religious circles, symbols and signs seem to be really important. Starting with the ones which are considered most sacred, such as priestly robes and clerical collars, to perhaps more frivolous ones, such as pins and bumper stickers, religious Christianity is flooded with symbols. Some symbols are important and have validity: for instance, the cross and the fish have been used since the early days of the church. However, the Bible puts much more emphasis on our spiritual walk and on our behavior. After all, what good is a bumper sticker that says "honk if you love Jesus", if I am zooming along zig-zagging lane to lane, repeatedly honking at cars in front of me to get out of my way? It seems that the best signs that prove that we are genuine Christians are spiritual rather than physical. Instead of angrily flashing my headlights, I should let my inward light shine. Whenever I exhibit the fruit of the spirit, and I am kind and gentle with others, I don't need a bumper sticker or a pin on my chest to show that I am the real deal. The proof is in how I talk, how I walk, how I dress, and how I live. Friends, the best way to let our light shine is by our godly behavior and our good works. Jesus said that we must let those qualities shine brightly for all to see (Matt. 5:16). And when those qualities are evident, even though we may not be wearing any star-shaped brooches or pins, every time we walk into a room we will light it up with the glory of God. Those who see us will have no doubt that we are sincere followers of Christ and, thanks to our example, they will want to join us in following Him!

***The Lord, Jesus, the Word and the Holy Spirit are my light!***

# Chapter 3
# Salvation

## Rescued every time

Throughout our text, David uses words like "light, salvation, fortress" and, in other passages, he uses terms like "refuge, feathers, wings, shield, buckler, horn." In theology, these terms, and others like them, are called *anthropomorphisms.* They are limited, finite, human expressions which we use in our attempt to describe an unlimited, infinite, supernatural God.

To clarify, let's cite a couple of examples. To begin with, the Bible records that the "finger" of God wrote the ten commandments on tablets of stone.[14] Obviously, this does not mean that a giant finger from the sky appeared and inscribed those words on stone; rather, it means that God Himself is the Author of His law. Furthermore, it is written that the "hand of the Lord" came upon the prophet Ezekiel.[15] Again, this does not imply that a literal giant hand from the sky was on top of Ezekiel's head: it simply means that Yahweh's presence, His anointing, was on Ezekiel's life in a special way. Lastly, the book of Psalms declares that the Lord will cover us with His "feathers".[16] Once again, this does not mean that God literally has "feathers"; rather, it simply means that He will protect us like a mother hen protects her chicks.[17]

---

14) Exodus 31:18
15) Ezekiel 3:14
16) Psalms 91:4
17) Matthew 23:37 "O Jerusalem, Jerusalem, the city that kills the prophets and stones God's messengers! How often I have wanted to gather your children together as a hen protects her chicks beneath her wings, but you wouldn't let me.

Almighty God, the all-powerful Creator of the universe, has chosen to interact with limited, indeed very limited, human beings. Anthropomorphisms greatly help us in describing our invisible God, and in relating in comprehensible terms His relationship with us.

The bottom line is that many times David used representative language: God is our Shepherd because He makes us lie down in green pastures so we can eat, He leads us besides still waters so we can drink, He restores our souls so we can be refreshed, He uses His rod to protect us.[18]

Anthropomorphisms help us understand that God is whatever we need, no matter what circumstance we find ourselves in: if we are hungry, He is bread; if we are thirsty, He is water;[19] if we are wavering, He is our Rock, our stability;[20] if we are sick, He is our Physician;[21] if we have needs, He is our Provider.[22]

Now that we are a little better equipped to understand the symbolisms that David uses, let us continue in our meditation.

**Psalms 27:1 The Lord is my light and my salvation—so why should I be afraid? The Lord is my fortress, protecting me from danger, so why should I tremble?**

---

18) See Psalms 23
19) John 6:35 Jesus replied, "I am the bread of life. Whoever comes to me will never be hungry again. Whoever believes in me will never be thirsty
20) Deuteronomy 32:4 He is the Rock; his deeds are perfect. Everything he does is just and fair. He is a faithful God who does no wrong; how just and upright he is!
21) Exodus 15:26 ...I am the LORD ·who heals you [your physician]." (Expanded Bible)
22) Philippians 4:19 And my God shall supply all your need according to His riches in glory by Christ Jesus. (NKJV)

In this verse, not only does King David declare that the Lord is His light, but he goes on to proclaim that He is his salvation. The word translated "salvation" is the Hebrew term *yesha*, and it means "to save from evils and troubles."[23] This means that God rescues us whenever we find ourselves in difficult situations. Whatever we need to be rescued from, whatever we need help with, the Lord is our way out. If He rescued David, He will also rescue us.

Paul, who had the same spirit of faith as David,[24] also believed that God was his salvation in times of trouble:

**2 Corinthians 1:9 In fact, we expected to die. But as a result, we stopped relying on ourselves and learned to rely only on God, who raises the dead.**

In this passage, Paul clearly states that he was in danger of dying. Both King David and the apostle Paul faced many challenges and dangers in their service for God. Neither one of them ever hid or minimized the problems they experienced: on the contrary, they were transparent and wrote openly about the challenges they encountered.

However, Paul and David didn't just state that they had problems and left it at that. I am saying that they did not simply make a list of the woes and sorrows of life; rather, they went on to express their firm trust in God and in His ability to rescue them. Note what Paul says in the next verse:

---

23) Brown, F., Driver, S. R., & Briggs, C. A. (1977). *Enhanced Brown-Driver-Briggs Hebrew and English Lexicon* (pp. 446–447). Oxford: Clarendon Press.
24) 2 Corinthians 4:13 And since we have the same spirit of faith, according to what is written, "I believed and therefore I spoke," we also believe and therefore speak (NKJV).

**2 Corinthians 1:10 And he did rescue us from mortal danger, and he will rescue us again. We have placed our confidence in him, and he will continue to rescue us.**

Paul stated emphatically that God was faithful in rescuing him. The apostle expressed firm confidence in God's saving ability. He used the word "confidence", just like David did in verse 3 of Psalm 27.[25]

Look the New King James translation of this verse:

**2 Corinthians 1:10 who delivered us from so great a death, and does deliver us; in whom we trust that He will still deliver *us*,**

Paul declared that God *delivered* him (past tense), that He *does deliver* him (present tense), and that He will *still deliver* him (future tense). In other words, God rescued him in the past and in the present, and Paul was convinced that He would continue to do the same in the future.

The Bible makes it clear that when we walk with God we will face many challenges:

**Psalms 34:19 The righteous person faces many troubles...**

We know first-hand that this verse is absolutely true: those who follow God will face *many troubles*. Many precious servants of God have earned an advanced degree from the University of Hard Knocks. However, it's vital to note that this is only the first part of the verse. Let's see what the rest of the verse says:

---

25) Psalms 27:3 Though a mighty army surrounds me, my heart will not be afraid. Even if I am attacked, I will remain confident. (NLT).

**Psalms 34:19 The righteous person faces many troubles, but the Lord comes to the rescue each time.**

Now, if the first part of the verse is true (the *"many troubles"*), then the second part must also be true (the *"rescue"*). It would be theologically unsound, not to mention totally illogical, to believe only half a verse! If it's true that we face many troubles, it must be equally true that the Lord comes to the rescue each time.

The Expanded Bible brings out another interesting shade of meaning:

**Psalms 34:19 People who ·do what is right may [are righteous] have many ·problems [afflictions], but the LORD ·will solve them [saves them from them] all. (Expanded Bible)**

The Lord will solve *them*, meaning the Lord will solve *the problems*. This translation expresses David's words in terms of solutions to problems. The concepts we are studying are not for people who attempt to solve things using only their own strength. When it comes to the important issues of life, the Bible does not advocate a *do-it-yourself* approach, which is usually found in most books that clutter up the *self-help* section of bookstores. The principles outlined in the Bible are for all those who believe in God and in His power. They are for those who, borrowing the terminology of the Amplified Bible, *"adhere to, trust in, and rely on"* God for things to work out.[26] Thank God that He is reliable

---

26) Romans 10:9 Because if you acknowledge and confess with your lips that Jesus is Lord and in your heart believe (adhere to, trust in, and rely on the truth) that God raised Him from the dead, you will be saved. (AMP)

and we can depend on Him to rescue us every single time we need it!

Paul himself, at the end of his earthly life, declared that he had faced many dangers and challenges, but the Lord had been faithful and rescued him out of them all:

**2 Timothy 3:10-11 But you, Timothy, certainly know what I teach, and how I live, and what my purpose in life is. You know my faith, my patience, my love, and my endurance. [11] You know how much persecution and suffering I have endured. You know all about how I was persecuted in Antioch, Iconium, and Lystra—but the Lord rescued me from all of it.**

Look at the last phrase: "the Lord rescued me from all of it." Not just *some* of it, but *all* of it.

God did this for King David, He did it for the apostle Paul, and He will do it for all who trust in Him.

***The Lord is my light and my salvation!***

# Chapter 4
# Fortress

## Simply impregnable

In two passages of Scripture, David is described as a "man after God's own heart."[27] King David had an intimate, intense relationship with the Lord. He was totally dedicated to Him. Spiritually speaking, David was way ahead of his time. In Chapter 9, we will see precisely why this is so, and we will also attempt to probe his mind. For now, suffice it to say that he had a unique way of thinking. David really liked to magnify God. Here is one example of this:

**Psalms 34:3 Oh, magnify the Lord with me, And let us exalt His name together.**

*Magnifying* basically means *"enlarging."*[28] After all, a magnifying glass makes things look bigger. Some think that applying this concept to God or to human beings almost sounds like exaggeration: it is not. Magnifying is not exaggerating. When we exaggerate, we enlarge beyond the truth and we add things that are not there. Exaggeration is in essence a form of lying. In contrast to this, magnifying is enlarging what is truly there so it can be seen better. There is no lying in magnifying. For example, when a scientist magnifies a cell under a microscope, he or she is not adding anything to the cell. The nucleus, membrane, chromosomes and all the other components he observes, really do exist.

---

27) 1 Samuel 13:14; Acts 13:22
28) Merriam-Webster. (2008). Merriam-Webster's 11th Collegiate Dictionary. Fogware Publishing, Art Software Inc. and Data Storage Research LLC.

He is simply doing something to see them better, so that he can accurately describe what is already there.

David's praise was like a magnifying glass and it helped him see God more clearly and understand Him better. When he lifted his voice and proclaimed "Praise the Lord, for His mercy endures forever,"[29] and repeated it over and over again, He is magnifying a genuine aspect of God's character. David is not declaring this to make it a reality, he is declaring it because it is a reality: God's mercy really does endure forever. David is not exaggerating, he is magnifying.

Not only does magnifying God help us understand Him better, it also produces another important benefit. The more God is magnified, the smaller everything else becomes. In our text, as David magnifies God and makes Him bigger and bigger, his problems become that much smaller. Concerning this, the Expositor's Bible Commentary explains that, "regardless of how great the adversities, the psalmist looks at the greatness of the Lord in relation to the insignificance of his own problems."[30] This means that all of David's fears, all the people who opposed him, all the armies who surrounded him became small and insignificant in comparison to how big and powerful God really is. In David's heart, even Goliath the giant became small in comparison to the Lord of Hosts, the Lord of the Armies of Heaven![31]

Let's look at what the prophet Isaiah wrote:

---

29) Psalms 136
30) Gaebelein, Frank E. (Jun 15, 2016, 11:50:43 PDT). *Expositor's Bible Commentary (12 Vols)*. Zondervan.
31) 1 Samuel 17:45 David replied to the Philistine, "You come to me with sword, spear, and javelin, but I come to you in the name of the Lord of Heaven's Armies—the God of the armies of Israel, whom you have defied.

**Isaiah 40:4 Every valley shall be exalted And every mountain and hill brought low; The crooked places shall be made straight And the rough places smooth;**

Mountains and hills will be brought low. We know that the ultimate fulfillment of this verse will be in the Day of the Lord. However, when we praise and magnify God, we can have a foretaste of mountains and hills shrinking. When we place our trust in God, mountains become molehills.

Try it sometime: praise God, magnify Him, make Him really big, and you too will see how small and insignificant the problems you are facing will become compared to the all-loving, all-present, all-knowing, all-powerful God you serve.

Let's take the reflection we just made on magnifying the Lord and apply it to the next sentence in our text:

**Psalms 27:1 The Lord is my light and my salvation—so why should I be afraid? The Lord is my fortress, protecting me from danger, so why should I tremble?**

The Lord is our fortress. David is using strong images not only to describe just how powerful the Lord is, but also to expresses unflinching confidence in his God.

The Hebrew word translated "fortress" is *maoz*; it literally means "a stronghold, a fortified place".[32] In other words, as the Lexham Theological Wordbook puts it, our God is an unassailable provider of safety and protection.[33]

---

32) Strong, J. (1995). *Enhanced Strong's Lexicon*. Woodside Bible Fellowship.
33) Smith, W. A. (2014). Protection. D. Mangum, D. R. Brown, R. Klippenstein, & R. Hurst (Eds.), *Lexham Theological Wordbook*. Bellingham, WA: Lexham Press.

A fortress provides refuge and protection. A fortress is not just any castle: it is a fortified stronghold, usually located in a high place. Many years ago, a movie came out entitled *Where the Eagles Dare*, starring Clint Eastwood, Richard Burton and other famous actors. As the film synopsis puts it, a crack team of Allied soldiers staged a daring rescue during World War II. A U.S. general was being held captive in an imposing fortress high in the Bavarian Alps, and the soldiers had to get him out. Now that's a very good way of describing a fortress!

Citing more authoritative sources, in his commentary John Walton explains that in ancient times some fortresses had strong defenses and adequate supplies of food and water which enabled them to endure lengthy sieges. Certain strongholds were so well supplied that they were able to withstand an attack indefinitely.[34]

My wife and I have been serving God for more than thirty-six years. In all these years, God has always provided everything our family has ever needed. By His grace, we never had to skip a meal or a rent payment, and we always had clothes on our backs. Thank God for His amazing grace and His unfailing faithfulness!

Let me be frank: there have been times in our lives when it *looked like* we were not going to make it. Way back in the late 1970s, at the height of the Disco fever, Connie and I started out with a small Bible study in the basement of a friend's house. We quickly outgrew that location, and we

---

34) Walton, John. (Jul 7, 2016, 10:33:01 PDT). *Illustrated Bible Backgrounds Commentary of the Old Testament (5 Vols)*. Zondervan.

moved to a friend's banquet hall. After a few months, we outgrew the hall and, in obedience to the Lord, we rented our first building. It was an old bank, and it needed to be renovated. This was a huge step of faith. At that time, in addition to pastoring our small congregation, Connie and I were attending university, and on top of that we both had part-time jobs. We literally poured every cent of our modest salaries into the church. We were not tithing, we were *one-hundred-percenting*: we were not giving just 10% of our income to the church, we were giving all of it! In those early formative days of ministry, the enemy attacked us and tried to destroy our young church. There were times when *it looked like* we were not going to make it to the end of the month. The adversary, that is the devil, put us under siege, but the Lord was our fortress and by His grace we were able to withstand all kinds of financial pressure. As the years passed, we progressed to even bigger buildings, the expenses naturally kept on increasing, and again there were times when it looked like we did not have the resources to make it. I remember two times in particular when it came right down to the wire, but the Lord continued to be our fortress, impregnable and full of inexhaustible provisions. He came through every single time.

The God who lifted Joseph out of the pit and out of the prison, is the same God who brought us from the basement, to the banquet hall, to the bank and to the warehouse. He is finishing what He started.[35] And since He is the one that started the work, He will supply all that is needed. He *is* our fortress.

---

35) Philippians 1:6 being confident of this very thing, that He who has begun a good work in you will complete it until the day of Jesus Christ. (NKJV)

If you have walked with God any length of time, I am sure that your testimony is similar to ours. His grace extends to all His children. You too have lived through times where you thought you would not make it, but the Lord is your fortress: you took refuge in Him, He sheltered you during the siege and He supplied enough resources so that you could make it. This is exactly what the apostle Paul believed and declared:

**Philippians 4:19 And this same God who takes care of me will supply all your needs from his glorious riches, which have been given to us in Christ Jesus.**

God will supply all our needs. The previous phrase was not coined by some modern-day, positive-thinking motivational preacher: the Holy Spirit inspired the apostle Paul to write it. It follows that this cannot be an extreme, cultish doctrine; quite the contrary: this is orthodox, New Testament Christianity. The fact that God blesses His people and He supplies their needs is a well-established Bible truth, found in both the Old and New Testaments.

The Amplified translation is simply delightful:

**Philippians 4:19 And my God will liberally supply (fill to the full) your every need according to His riches in glory in Christ Jesus. (AMP)**

God will liberally supply and fill to the full our every need! God in His Word promised us this. Let's take Him seriously. Let's take Him at His Word.

***The Lord is my light, my salvation and my fortress!***

# Chapter 5
# Fear

## No fear of any kind

Let's now turn our attention to other portions of verse 1 which we have not yet covered:

**Psalms 27:1 The Lord is my light and my salvation—so why should I be afraid? The Lord is my fortress, protecting me from danger, so why should I tremble?**

David asks two questions: why should I be afraid? Why should I tremble? Notice that he uses two different words for "fear".

The first word, "afraid", is the Hebrew word *yare*. This is the most common word used for fear. The second word, however, is different. The word translated "tremble" is the Hebrew word *pachad*.[36] That's why the NLT rightly uses two different words in its English translation, "*afraid*" and "*tremble*". The term "afraid" implies the concept of generic fear, while "trembling" denotes a more specific fear. The latter term describes some specific occurrence that startles us and makes us *tremble*. For instance, a sudden noise at nighttime, a near miss with another car at an intersection, or running into a hungry grizzly bear while hiking in the Rocky Mountains. Events like these would definitely shake us up and make us tremble.

---

36) Strong, J. (1995). *Enhanced Strong's Lexicon.* Woodside Bible Fellowship.

The EBC commentary remarks that using two different words for fear exude an expression of strong confidence in the Lord.[37] David's point is that whether we are talking about generalized anxiety or specific fears, either way the Lord is our light, our salvation and our fortress. So we are definitely not afraid. *Never.*

In another Psalm, David boldly declared:

**Psalms 34:4 I prayed to the Lord, and he answered me. He freed me from all my fears.**

The apostle Paul concurs:

**2 Timothy 1:7 For God has not given us a spirit of fear, but of power and of love and of a sound mind. (NKJV)**

Upon careful examination of the above Scriptures the undeniable conclusion is that the Lord has freed us from *all* our fears: generalized anxiety, specific fears, small fears, and even large pathological phobias. He delivered us out of them all!

Hold on to your seat, here is the Amplified translation:

**2 Timothy 1:7 For God did not give us a spirit of timidity (of cowardice, of craven and cringing and fawning fear), but [He has given us a spirit] of power and of love and of calm and well-balanced mind and discipline and self-control. (AMP)**

So, not only have we been set free from all fears, but God has filled us with His power and love, and He has given

---

37) Gaebelein, Frank E. (Jun 15, 2016, 11:50:43 PDT). *Expositor's Bible Commentary* (12 Vols). Zondervan.

us a calm, well-balanced mind, discipline and self-control. Based on what the Bible says, there doesn't seem to be any reason why we should ever be anxious or panic.

*The Lord is my light.* Let's conclude this chapter by talking some more about light. It is not a coincidence that David used this anthropomorphism. Since all Scripture is breathed by God, we know that he must have been inspired by the Holy Spirit.[38] But why would He inspire the use of this imagery? What is so special about light?

This is not an easy question to answer. For millennia, mankind has been fascinated by light and baffled by its nature. Suffice it to say that light is quite unique and powerful.

Light is fast, incomprehensibly fast, it travels at 299,792 km/sec (186,272 miles/sec). This is lighting fast. To help us wrap our heads around this, someone gave the following illustration: if I had a gun armed with a bullet which could travel at the speed of light and I fired it straight ahead towards the horizon, before I could remove my finger from the trigger the bullet would travel seven times around the circumference of the earth and whiz by me an equal number of times.[39]

Let's indulge in two more illustrations. First, for the sake of argument, let's round off the speed of light to 300,000 km/sec. The moon is 384,400 km away from the earth,

---

38) 2 Timothy 3:16 Every Scripture is God-breathed (given by His inspiration) and profitable for instruction… (AMP)
39) Redd, Nola Taylor. "How fast does light travel?" SPACE.com. https://www.space.com/15830-light-speed.html (accessed June 23, 2017).

which means that it takes approximately one second for a photon to travel from one to the other. How would you like to take one step from wherever you are right now and find yourself on the moon?

Our second, and final illustration on this topic. Generally speaking, we travel in cars at 100 km/h (55 miles/h), in jets at 700 km/h (500 miles/h), and in rockets at 1,200 km/h (760 miles/h). We think that this is fast. However, light travels at the phenomenal speed of 1080 million km/h (670,000,000 miles/h). In other words, in my car in one hour I travel 100 km (55 miles), while in the same amount of time light has travelled 1080 million km. Yes, more than *one thousand million kilometres*. Which basically means that in one hour a photon has travelled well outside of our Solar System!

It's important to specify that visible, or natural light, is *not* God; rather, it is a *creation* of God. When the Bible states that "God is light", it does not mean that God is physical light. The latter was created by the former. We already saw in Chapter 1 that physical light is separate and distinct from the light of God. God personally kept the earth lit for three days with His presence before He created the light of the sun. God is a different kind of light, infinitely more powerful than the light He created.

Why the brief lesson in physics? Simple: to make the point that light is extremely powerful, and God is the One who created it. Can we even begin to comprehend how powerful God really is?

Even though the authors of Scripture knew nothing of modern physics, they were still able to observe light from

36

sources familiar to them, such as the sun, the stars and fires. Light was among the most powerful and compelling phenomenon they could observe. In inspiring them to use the phrase "God is light", the Holy Spirit was revealing to them that the God who created light was infinitely powerful. They had no computers or tablets, yet they came to the same conclusion as we do.

Do you see how the Bible is still a current book? Even though humans have made great advancements in science, we are still fascinated by the concept of light. To this day light is not fully understood and it still represents something extremely powerful. Friend, the Word of God is not outdated. In reality, the Bible is a relevant book for today, filled with practical wisdom to guide us in our relationship with God and in our interactions with other human beings.

Let's continue by looking at some more properties of light, both physically and spiritually speaking.

Naturally speaking, light dispels darkness; spiritually speaking, light dispels fear. Going back to our earlier analogy of a dark room, when we don't see what is around us we could be afraid. But when we turn on the light, all fear dissipates because we can plainly see what is around us.

Light is an entity that automatically dispels darkness. *It always does*. This also is true from both a natural and a spiritual perspective. In the following verse, this is exactly what John is talking about:

**John 1:5 The light shines in the darkness, and the darkness can never extinguish it.**

Spiritual darkness could not extinguish the spiritual light of God. Darkness can *never* extinguish light. No matter how thick the darkness is, turning on even the smallest of lights causes it to dissipate. It has no choice. Notice how the Amplified version translates this same verse:

> **John 1:5 And the Light shines on in the darkness, for the darkness has never overpowered it [put it out or absorbed it or appropriated it, and is unreceptive to it]. (AMP)**

Darkness can never overpower or put out light. No evil in the world, no enemy, no wicked person can hurt us or overcome us.

Remarkably, when God decides to shine His light on someone, that person becomes powerful in the Lord. And God can choose to shine a light on whomever or whatever He wants. He shone His light on a donkey, and the donkey spoke,[40] on a jawbone, and Samson used it to kill 1,000 enemies,[41] on five loaves and two fish, and that became enough to feed five thousand people.[42]

Saul of Tarsus was obsessed with eradicating Christianity from the face of the earth. He tried to do this by persecuting the Church and by killing as many Christians as he possibly could. One day he was on the road to Damascus, busy doing what he enjoyed best: chaining up believers and dragging them to Jerusalem. But this particular day turned out to be different, and something unusual happened: God decided to shine His light on him. This was enough to paralyze his escort and, more importantly, drive all darkness out of Saul's heart:

---

40) Numbers 22:28
41) Judges 15:15
42) John 6:10

**Acts 9:3-4 As he was approaching Damascus on this mission, a light from heaven suddenly shone down around him. ⁴ He fell to the ground and heard a voice saying to him, "Saul! Saul! Why are you persecuting me?" (NLT)**

God's light was so powerful that it set a number of unstoppable events into motion: the immediate effect was that Saul was knocked off his horse, the short-term effect was that he could not see for three days, and the long-term effects were that he was converted, his name was changed to Paul, and God turned him into the greatest apostle of all time.

One more illustration of what happens when God shines His light in someone's life. The book of Acts records that King Herod Agrippa imprisoned Peter and placed him under the guard of four squads of soldiers:

**Acts 12:4 Then he imprisoned him, placing him under the guard of four squads of four soldiers each. Herod intended to bring Peter out for public trial after the Passover. (NLT)**

In response to the prayers of His Church,[43] God shone His light on that jail cell:

**Acts 12:7 Suddenly, there was a bright light in the cell, and an angel of the Lord stood before Peter. The angel struck him on the side to awaken him and said, "Quick! Get up!" And the chains fell off his wrists. (NLT)**

What ensued was a spectacular, supernatural jailbreak. It was a divine chain reaction: God's light was powerful enough to wake Peter up, knock out the soldiers guarding him, break off the chains that bound him, and get him out of jail.

***The Lord is my light, my salvation and my fortress; therefore, I will not fear!***

---

43) Acts 12:5 But while Peter was in prison, the church prayed very earnestly for him.

# Chapter 6
# Enemies and adversaries

### *They work for you*

So far, we have studied the first verse of the twenty-seventh Psalm, which talks about light and freedom from all kinds of fears. As we move on to the next verse we see David shifting from inward to outward problems.

David begins verse 2 by talking about people who want to hurt him:

**Psalms 27:2 When evil people come to devour me, when my enemies and foes attack me, they will stumble and fall.**

In life, not only do we have to grapple with inward struggles, we also have to deal with outward ones. Unfortunately, there are times when we go through adverse circumstances and times when we face people who oppose us. These are not internal issues; they are external ones.

I don't know about you but many years ago, when I had just started my walk with God, I thought that eventually I would become so "spiritual" that I would no longer have any conflicts with other people. Well, I have been serving God 36 years and that day has not yet come! To this day I am still learning how to better manage difficult people.

Thinking that eventually one day we reach the point where we will no longer face any challenges does not correspond to reality. It is not Bible thinking: it is wishful thinking.

It is easy to demonstrate how faulty this way of thinking is. Virtually all Christians agree that a person cannot be more spiritual than Jesus. Jesus was, and is, absolutely perfect; yet in His earthly life He also had to deal with people who opposed Him. On the one hand, He was surrounded by religious people who constantly contrasted Him, while on the other hand His proud disciples were arguing over who was the greatest among them. Furthermore, Jesus had to deal with Peter who denied Him and Judas who betrayed Him. In the end, a wicked humanity nailed Him to a cross and killed Him. It seems obvious that Jesus had people problems from His first to His last day on earth.

The point is that no matter how spiritually mature we become, and how skilled and tactful we are in our interactions with other people, chances are that we will continue to encounter people who oppose us. Sadly, at times we may even encounter people who may want to harm us. That is exactly what was happening in David's life at the time he wrote the twenty-seventh Psalm. Using his own words, there were "evil people" trying to devour him.

Notice that in our text David makes a distinction between "enemies" and "foes". In our study, instead of "foe", we will use the word *adversary*; it's more contemporary. There is a subtle distinction between an "enemy" and an "adversary". Both are in opposition but, generally speaking, an enemy is more wicked than an adversary. The former intends to do more harm than the latter. An "adversary" is a more polite way to describe an "enemy". For instance, we don't label as "enemies" those who belong to another political party; rather, we call them "adversaries". Similarly, we don't call players from a rival sport team "enemies": we refer to them as "adversaries". Adversaries usually wear uniforms, while this is not always true concerning enemies. This means that at times an enemy can be right in our midst, making him all that much harder to identify. Let's remember that Judas was one of the twelve apostles, yet he betrayed Jesus. Judas had supper with Jesus just before he stabbed him in the back. That's what enemies do.

At this juncture, if we are true followers of Jesus, all this talk about enemies, adversaries and wars (more about this in the next chapter) should make us a little uncomfortable. True born again believers are peace-loving, non-violent people. After all, Jesus is called the Prince of Peace.[44]

Yet David talked about evil people, enemies, and adversaries. He was literally facing them - and he is not alone in this: the apostle Paul faced people who opposed him, just like you and I have done at certain times in our lives. The question now becomes: how do we handle enemies when we are called to live in peace?

We solve this apparent dilemma by understanding who our real enemy is. When it comes to dealing with difficult people, Paul helps us understand that there is more to this than meets the eye:

---

44) Isaiah 9:6 For a child is born to us, a son is given to us. The government will rest on his shoulders. And he will be called: Wonderful Counselor, Mighty God, Everlasting Father, Prince of Peace.

**Ephesians 6:11-12 Put on the whole armor of God, that you may be able to stand against the wiles of the devil. ¹² For we do not wrestle against flesh and blood, but against principalities, against powers, against the rulers of the darkness of this age, against spiritual hosts of wickedness in the heavenly places.**

We are not fighting against flesh and blood; this means that we are not fighting against people. People are not our problem. The real problem, the real enemy, is a spiritual one. So, while David was literally facing evil people, the real enemy was an invisible spiritual being called the devil.

So, as true followers of Jesus, how exactly do we deal with difficult people? Jesus lays out clearly what our course of action should be:

**Matthew 5:44 But I say to you, love your enemies, bless those who curse you, do good to those who hate you, and pray for those who spitefully use you and persecute you. (NKJV)**

Wow! Without a doubt, this is easier said than done. We are called to love everyone, including our enemies; not only that, but we are also instructed to do them good and to pray for them! This is one of the greatest revelations of New Testament Christianity. Naturally speaking, I can handle loving my enemies and praying for them, but *doing* good to those who are trying to hurt me stretches my mind and heart to the limit.

The apostle Paul gave similar instructions to the believers in Rome:

**Romans 12:17 Never pay back evil with more evil. Do things in such a way that everyone can see you are honorable.**

Don't repay evil with evil. Don't retaliate.

He continues:

**Romans 12:18 Do all that you can to live in peace with everyone.**

We are called to live in peace with everyone. Whether or not others do their part, we must do our part to be at peace with everyone.

Then Paul goes on to say:

**Romans 12:19-20 Dear friends, never take revenge. Leave that to the righteous anger of God. For the Scriptures say, "I will take revenge; I will pay them back," says the Lord.**
**[20] Instead, "If your enemies are hungry, feed them. If they are thirsty, give them something to drink. In doing this, you will heap burning coals of shame on their heads."**

We are not supposed to take revenge. So much for every Hollywood movie where the plot is all about revenge and getting even! We should let God avenge us. When someone treats us wrong, we trust Him to vindicate us. Let God set the record straight.

Does this mean that we allow bullies to step all over us and do what they want? No, it does not. We are not doormats. Look at how Paul concludes his thought on this subject:

**Romans 12:21 Don't let evil conquer you, but conquer evil by doing good.**

Evil will not conquer us; we will conquer it – and we will do it *with good*. When it comes to our enemies, we set boundaries as needed, love them, pray for them, even do them good and as we do that, the Lord takes care of us and protects us. In the end, we win.

The philosophy of life taught by Jesus is not a losing proposition: it is a winning one. We are victors, not victims. God wants us to have a positive, winning mindset. We pray for victory, not defeat. David prayed that God would not allow his enemies to triumph over him:

**Psalms 25:2 O my God, I trust in You; Let me not be ashamed; Let not my enemies triumph over me.**

In similar fashion the apostle Paul, referring to people who were trying to hurt him, made a powerful declaration:

**2 Corinthians 2:14 Now thanks be to God who always leads us in triumph in Christ, and through us diffuses the fragrance of His knowledge in every place.**

In Christ, we don't lose, we win. It's simply wonderful to know that no matter how hard the circumstances may seem, and no matter who is trying to hurt us, God promised that in Christ we always triumph. This is why we are not afraid of what people may do to us!

How does what we just discussed concerning walking in love tie into to our text? Let's look at it again attentively:

**Psalms 27:2 When evil people come to devour me, when my enemies and foes attack me, they will stumble and fall.**

Do you see it? The verse says that "they" will stumble and fall. They came to make David fall, but instead *they* fell. This applies to us too: people may come against us to try to make us fall, but in the end *they* will stumble and fall. Jamieson, Fausset and Brown, commenting on this verse, point out that the word "they" is emphatic. Not *I*, but *they* stumbled, they fell.[45] It was a loud thump.

Upon further reflection, it becomes clear that David was not the one who made them fall. The Lord took care of it. In the final analysis, here is the way it works: we pray for our enemies, meanwhile God works behind the scenes to vindicate us. And when He does, it will be public: everyone will see it. God did it for David, He did it for Joseph, and He will also do it for us.

It's kind of like the martial art known as Jujutsu. According to Wikipedia, "Ju" can be translated to mean "gentle, soft, supple, flexible, pliable, or yielding." "Jutsu" can be translated to mean "art" or "technique" and represents manipulating the opponent's force against himself rather than confronting it with one's own force.[46] This is the art of defeating enemies without resorting to violence. Spiritually speaking, we defeat our enemies without lifting a finger against them.

What they sow, they reap (which happens to be true for all of us in every aspects of life). It's a boomerang effect. The ill-will they exhibit against you will turn on them. You

---

45) Jamieson, R., Fausset, A. R., & Brown, D. (Jun 10, 2016, 22:43:50 PDT). *Jamieson, Fausset, and Brown Commentary.* Public Domain.
46) "Jujutsu." Wikipedia.org. https://en.wikipedia.org/wiki/Jujutsu (accessed June 16, 2017).

obey God, you are loving, you are gentle, you pray for them - and *they* fall.

There is another way to express the great Bible truth we just discussed.

When we walk with God, problems *cannot* stop us and *cannot* separate us from Him. We will study this in detail later in Chapter 10, but now is a good time to mention the one thing that problems do. Here is what one of the best-known verses in the Bible says about this:

**Romans 8:28 And we know that God causes everything to work together for the good of those who love God and are called according to his purpose for them.**

Evil clearly comes to hurt us but when we are called according to His purpose, when we are in the will of God, He steps in and causes bad things to work for our good. God turns the table around in our favour. Let's look at one example.

Job is the most ancient book in the Bible. In this great book, God sets the record straight. Right off the bat, He let mankind know that He is the one who rescues people in trouble, while Satan is the one who causes problems in their lives. Let's never confuse the two.

Note how Satan attacked Job:

**Job 2:7 So Satan went out from the presence of the Lord, and struck Job with painful boils from the sole of his foot to the crown of his head. (NKJV)**

Religion has always grappled with the question of evil and has formulated many wrong doctrines in its attempt to allocate blame for the existence of evil in the world. Too often religiosity has wrongly placed responsibility squarely on God's shoulders for many of the bad things that happen in people's lives. The verse we just read makes it clear that it was Satan that struck Job. Satan, not God, was responsible for all the evil things which occurred in his life. And what did God do? He did what He always does: He stepped into Job's troubled life and rescued him from the problems that Satan had caused. This becomes very clear at the end of the book:

**Job 42:10 And the Lord restored Job's losses when he prayed for his friends. Indeed the Lord gave Job twice as much as he had before. (NKJV)**

I really like the way the Amplified version translates this verse:

**Job 42:10 And the Lord turned the captivity of Job and restored his fortunes, when he prayed for his friends; also the Lord gave Job twice as much as he had before. (AMP)**

The Lord *turned* the captivity of Job. I see in this a picture of the boomerang effect we mentioned earlier. God took the evil that Satan threw at Job, turned it around and sent it back. In the end, instead of destruction Job got twice as much as he had before! God is good, isn't He?

What happened to Job proves that in a certain sense evil things actually work in our favour. Satan tried to take away all his possessions, but Satan's evil scheme backfired because Job ended up having much more that he had before.

We could say that when we walk with God our enemies actually work for us!

This is a well-established Bible truth: when we are in the will of God, there is no way the enemy can stop us from reaching our God-given destiny. In fact, whatever evil he throws our way will be turned around and will be used to get us to our destination faster.

This is what gave King David great confidence. He understood that no matter what the devil threw at him, not only would God deliver him every single time, but it would actually be used to move him closer to his destiny!

This is why in Psalm 27, and in many other Psalms, David often recounted how God constantly rescued him from all his past troubles. Each victory over his enemies helped him get closer and closer to his ultimate destiny: the throne in Jerusalem.

Let's make this point even clearer by looking at what David told King Saul concerning killing Goliath:

**1 Samuel 17:36 Your servant has killed both lion and bear; and this uncircumcised Philistine will be like one of them, seeing he has defied the armies of the living God."**

Killing the lion helped him learn how to kill the bear, which in turn helped him learn how to kill the giant. After that, David graduated to defeating whole armies and winning entire wars. Finally, he was crowned king of Israel.

In similar fashion, our next step in God rests on the

foundation of the previous battles we have won. Our next level of glory stands on the carcasses of lions, bears and giants we have defeated in the past.

Here are a couple more Scriptures to illustrate this all-important principle, that victories over enemies help us move forward in our walk with God. The first one is from the book of Exodus:

**Exodus 1:12 But the more the Egyptians oppressed them, the more the Israelites multiplied and spread, and the more alarmed the Egyptians became.**

The more the Egyptians oppressed the Israelites, the more the latter multiplied and spread. The enemy tried to crush them and instead they got stronger and stronger.

The second passage comes from the book of Genesis. If you recall, Joseph was intensely hated by his brothers. Their initial plan was to kill him and throw him in a pit:

**Genesis 37:20 "Come on, let's kill him and throw him into one of these cisterns. We can tell our father, 'A wild animal has eaten him.' Then we'll see what becomes of his dreams!"**

Realizing that there was no profit in this course of action, they sold him as a slave:

**Genesis 37:28 So when the Ishmaelites, who were Midianite traders, came by, Joseph's brothers pulled him out of the cistern and sold him to them for twenty pieces of silver. And the traders took him to Egypt.**

Joseph then went through many ups and downs, but God was with him and rescued him every single time. Eventually, he reached the high position of governor of Egypt.[47] He was second in command to Pharaoh.[48]

After some time, there was a severe recession, so some of his brothers went to see Joseph to ask for assistance. When they finally recognized him, they were afraid. Joseph reassured them that he was not going to harm them in any way:

**Genesis 50:21 No, don't be afraid. I will continue to take care of you and your children." So he reassured them by speaking kindly to them.**

Admittedly, this is a real show of maturity on Joseph's part. It's pure love. It is the kind of love that Jesus and Paul talked about: doing good to those who harm us. Is it any wonder that Joseph was blessed everywhere he went?[49]

Amid all this, Joseph also tells his brothers:

**Genesis 50:20 You intended to harm me, but God intended it all for good. He brought me to this position so I could save the lives of many people.**

Joseph knew that they had intended to hurt him, but God had different intentions. This is indeed a wonderful Bible truth.

---

47) Genesis 42:6 Since Joseph was governor of all Egypt and in charge of selling grain to all the people, it was to him that his brothers came. When they arrived, they bowed before him with their faces to the ground.
48) Genesis 41:40 You will be in charge of my court, and all my people will take orders from you. Only I, sitting on my throne, will have a rank higher than yours."
49) Genesis 39:2 The Lord was with Joseph, so he succeeded in everything he did as he served in the home of his Egyptian master.

Does this mean that God is the one that *causes* the devil to hurt us? Absolutely not! God is not evil. As we saw earlier in the life of Job, the devil is the troublemaker, not God. Jesus explained it best in the Gospel of John:

**John 10:10 The thief's purpose is to steal and kill and destroy. My purpose is to give them a rich and satisfying life.**

Anything that steals, kills and destroys comes from the evil one. Abundant life comes from God. James says it this way:

**James 1:16-17 So don't be misled, my dear brothers and sisters. 17 Whatever is good and perfect comes down to us from God our Father, who created all the lights in the heavens. He never changes or casts a shifting shadow.**

*Don't be misled.* It's easy to be confused about this, especially since there are plenty of wrong traditions of men that muddy up the waters.[50] In the Bible, things are clear: Satan, not God, stole, killed and destroyed in Job's life; God stepped in, rescued him, and blessed him with abundance.

In this great stage called life, all parties involved have clear roles and responsibilities: Satan causes evil, God rescues, man chooses between good and evil.[51]

Let's read again what Joseph said to his brothers:

---

50) Mark 7:13 making the word of God of no effect through your tradition which you have handed down. And many such things you do." (NKJV)
51) Deuteronomy 30:19 "Today I have given you the choice between life and death, between blessings and curses. Now I call on heaven and earth to witness the choice you make. Oh, that you would choose life, so that you and your descendants might live!

**Genesis 50:20 You intended to harm me, but God intended it all for good. He brought me to this position so I could save the lives of many people.**

*"You"* intended to harm me. Who intended to harm Joseph? His brothers. In other words, Joseph's brothers were guilty of throwing him in the pit and selling him as a slave. It was their responsibility, not God's. And they will be judged for what they did.

What did God intend? God intended to free Joseph from his brothers' evil intentions. God rescued Joseph and got him out of the pit; later on, He rescued him from Potiphar's wife and from prison. This is who He is and what He does: He steps into our lives and rescues us from evil. This is why He is called the Redeemer.[52]

Don't ever be afraid of people who reject you, oppose you, or hurt you. Don't be afraid of the dark in the world, because God is your light.

*The Lord is my light, my salvation and my fortress; therefore, I will not fear. No one can hurt me!*

---

52) Job 19:25 "But as for me, I know that my Redeemer lives, and he will stand upon the earth at last.

# Chapter 7
# Wars and armies

*When things get really hectic*

David starts the twenty-seventh Psalm talking about anxiety and fear, and then he moves on to enemies and adversaries. Clearly, there is an escalation. The problems are increasing, with both internal and external challenges.

Looking at the next verse, it becomes clear that the escalation continues:

**Psalms 27:3 Though an army may encamp against me, My heart shall not fear; Though war may rise against me, In this I will be confident.**

David is now talking about armies and wars! He has gone from inward fears, to enemies and adversaries, and finally to armies encamping against him and war breaking out against him.

As I mentioned in the last chapter, most of us would like to think that the more we grow spiritually, the easier things will become; we may even fantasize about the coming of a day when we will have no more problems for the rest of our lives. Friends, the only time this will happen is when we will go to heaven. As long as we are on this earth, we will face difficulties. In fact, the Bible seems to indicate that the more we walk with God, the bigger the challenges become.

This is exactly what happened in King David's life. If you recall, when he was facing the giant named Goliath,

David told King Saul that he would be able to kill the giant. Why? Because in the past he had already faced and successfully solved smaller problems. He had already slain the lion and the bear:

> **1 Samuel 17:34-35 But David said to Saul, "Your servant used to keep his father's sheep, and when a lion or a bear came and took a lamb out of the flock, [35] I went out after it and struck it, and delivered the lamb from its mouth; and when it arose against me, I caught it by its beard, and struck and killed it.**

Do you see the progression in David's life? First he killed a lion, then a bear, then a giant, and then he progressed to winning against whole armies. The more he walked with God, the more he grew, and the bigger the problems became. However, bigger battles meant bigger victories. The same is true in our lives: first we overcome inward fears, then we learn how to deal with difficult people, finally we learn how to solve even greater problems.

At this point, it's important to point out that even though David was talking about literal armies, the meaning is much broader than that. Let me explain what I mean. We already saw in the last chapter that we are not fighting against people. The real enemy is the devil.

Taking this a step further, the apostle Paul tells us that many passages in the Old Testament are "examples written for our admonition".[53] In other words, many Bible passages have both a literal, natural application and a more symbolic,

---

53) 1 Corinthians 10:11 These things happened to them as examples for us. They were written down to warn us who live at the end of the age.

spiritual application. In our text, David was facing a literal army, but there is more to it than that. Let's see what the broader, symbolic meaning is.

Facing an army is not like facing one or two individuals, because an army is a large body of persons trained and armed for war. Symbolically speaking, an "army" represents all kinds of problems - and lots of them. David also mentions war. In other words, he was facing a large number of organized enemies and he was attacked on all sides. It was all-out war. Clearly, this is symbolic language describing times in our lives when we are facing all kinds of difficulties and problems.

This is why the ESV study notes remark that in the 3rd verse of Psalm 27, David was cultivating confidence in God *"in the widest range of challenging life situations."*[54] In other words, the notes point out that the fears, individuals and armies taken together represent the many different kinds of challenges he was facing, and in each instance David was expressing great confidence in God.

It seems that in the modern times we are living in, humanity as a whole is facing problems on an unprecedented scale. There are inward and outward struggles, things are changing faster than they ever have before and we are uncertain about many things. Immorality is rampant, and the church is being attacked from the outside with persecution and from the inside with many strange doctrines. It's a constant barrage.

---

54) The Holy Bible, English Standard Version. (Jun 15, 2016, 13:41:16 PDT). *ESV Study Bible Notes.* Crossway.

On a more personal level, there are days when it seems like everything is going wrong: we wake up late for work, the washing machine breaks down, the dog runs away, the car does not start, we go for a check-up and the doctor orders further tests because he finds something unexpected in our body.

Our text talks about anxiety, inward fears, individuals out to get us, armies surrounding us, and all-out war - all kinds of problems. It seems like all hell is breaking loose. And in all these situations, David boldly declares "I will not fear". Simply put, when God is on our side nothing fazes us.

Now I don't want you to be anxious about the future. David literally said, "though war may rise against me". *May* rise. Let's thank God that life is *not* an endless succession of constant problems. These things don't have to happen: they may happen sometimes. And *if* they happen, we are neither worried nor afraid.

Let's go back to our text:

**Psalms 27:3 Though an army may encamp against me, My heart shall not fear; Though war may rise against me, In this I will be confident.**

Not only does David say, "my heart shall not fear", but he then goes on to declare: "in this I will be confident". Even if it looks like everything in my life is falling apart, *I am still confident*. What a reassuring contrast between "fear" and "confidence". Even though the problems were growing, his confidence was growing that much stronger.

Why is confidence so important? The book of Hebrews gives us the answer:

**Hebrews 10:35 Therefore do not cast away your confidence, which has great reward.**

Confidence has great reward. What reward?

**Hebrews 10:36 For you have need of endurance, so that after you have done the will of God, you may receive the promise.**

If we endure, we receive the promise. In other words, we are confident that if we persevere during difficult times, the promises of God will come to pass in our lives.

**Hebrews 6:12 ...do not become sluggish, but imitate those who through faith and patience inherit the promises.**

We do not want to become sluggish. Never give up, never quit. Rather, imitate those who through faith and patience inherit the promises. Faith, endurance and patience are three essential qualities that are needed in order for us to experience all the wonderful promises of God.

One more quality is needed to complete this picture: joy.

We don't walk by faith, endure and persevere while gritting our teeth: we do it with joy. These are the instructions James gives us in his epistle:

**James 1:2 Dear brothers and sisters, when troubles come your way, consider it an opportunity for great joy.**

James talks about troubles - all kinds of troubles. These would include anxiety, doubt, worry, family issues, strife, sickness, financial problems, etc.

James tells us to *consider* them opportunities for great joy. If we are honest with ourselves, we will readily admit that this is easier said than done. If I get a pink slip from work, I don't immediately jump for joy and shout "whoopee, praise the Lord, I've been fired". This is not a *natural* reaction. That's because it's a *supernatural* reaction. I have to focus and train myself to react that way on purpose. I have to jump and shout on purpose. When trouble comes my way, I consider it an opportunity for great joy. It is not automatically joy; rather, I have to *consider* it joy. I have to see it as joy on purpose.

Problems are not joyful in themselves. We don't like to suffer just for the sake of suffering. There is no joy in trouble. We have to *consider* it joy. And we have to do it on purpose:

**Philippians 4:4 Rejoice in the Lord always. Again I will say, rejoice!**

We rejoice *in the Lord*. The trouble is not joyful. Our joy is in the Lord. And we do it *always*. In all circumstances, whether they are favourable or unfavourable.

Why exactly do we rejoice? We already said that it's not because we like to suffer. Here is the real reason why we rejoice:

**James 1:3 For you know that when your faith is tested, your endurance has a chance to grow.**

59

When our faith is tested, our endurance grows. Remember, trouble works for us. Each time we persevere during difficult times, we are giving our patience a workout. Workouts are good because they make us stronger and boost our endurance.

What happens next?

**James 1:4 So let it grow, for when your endurance is fully developed, you will be perfect and complete, needing nothing.**

When our endurance develops, we will be perfect and complete, needing nothing. *Perfect, complete, needing nothing.* This means that we have no needs. Just like Job, remember? He persevered, and God gave him twice as much as he had before. In the end, he was perfect, complete, and lacked nothing.

I am not arbitrarily connecting James to Job. James himself was thinking of Job when he wrote his epistle. How do we know? Let's look at the last chapter of the epistle:

**James 5:11 Indeed we count them blessed who endure. You have heard of the perseverance of Job and seen the end intended by the Lord—that the Lord is very compassionate and merciful.**

So you see that it is James that associates endurance with Job. Job endured and he received the end intended by the Lord. Satan intended destruction, but the Lord had different intentions. His plan was victory, restoration and blessing.

And this did not happen when he died and went to heaven. Job experienced the reward of endurance in his lifetime. Now we understand why we can count troubles as joy!

This is the source of our confidence. Faith, endurance and joy have great reward. As Paul said, we are confident. We don't worry. Our faith is not a struggle: it's a rest.[55] We don't have to wonder whether God wants to rescue us or not. We don't have to struggle to receive what God has promised us. Here is why:

**2 Corinthians 1:20 For all the promises of God in Him are Yes, and in Him Amen, to the glory of God through us.**

We don't have to convince God to give us all the wonderful things He promised us in His Word. Jesus is God's "yes" to all His promises. Just trust Him, rest in Him, rejoice, praise Him, keep going in difficult times and His blessings will manifest in your life.

David lived this way approximately one thousand years before the apostle Paul walked on this earth. This was the king's philosophy:

**Psalms 27:3 Though an army may encamp against me, My heart shall not fear; Though war may rise against me, In this I will be confident.**

David is just as emphatic about external problems, as he is about all inward issues. Whether he had to deal with fears (v. 1), individuals who opposed him (v. 2) or all-out war (v. 3), in each of these instances he refused to fear and he

---

55) Hebrews 4:3 For we who have believed do enter that rest... (NKJV)

remained equally confident in God's ability to rescue him. Why? Because the LORD was his light.

Let's imitate King David. If ever we were surrounded by all kinds of problems, we too will not fear: we will be confident and we will rejoice and praise God.

*The Lord is my light, my salvation and my fortress; therefore, I will not fear. No one and no circumstance can hurt me!*

# Chapter 8
# Heavy lifting

## Lifted up above circumstances

In the remaining chapters of this book, we will unpack verses 4 to 6. Let's begin with the fourth verse:

**Psalms 27:4 One thing I have desired of the Lord, That will I seek: That I may dwell in the house of the Lord All the days of my life, To behold the beauty of the Lord, And to inquire in His temple.**

In this verse, King David talks about "the house of the LORD" and the "temple". What house and what temple is he referring to?

This important question will be answered in the next chapter. First, we must study the next two verses:

**Psalms 27:5 For in the time of trouble He shall hide me in His pavilion; In the secret place of His tabernacle He shall hide me; He shall set me high upon a rock.**

David states that God will first hide him in His pavilion and in the secret place of His tabernacle, and then He will set him high upon a rock.

When you are *high* upon a rock you are visible, but you are out of reach. This means that people who oppose you can't touch you. Evil around you can't harm you. Christ is our Rock, and Paul says that our life is hidden with Christ in God.[56]

---

56) Colossians 3:3 For you died, and your life is hidden with Christ in God. (NKJV)

There is an abrupt transition from the imagery of hiding to that of exposure on a rock. First we are hiding and no one can find us, then God sets us high upon a rock where everyone can see us. How does this work exactly?

This verse is a metaphor for David's life. First he was hidden, then he was lifted up. When David was a young man, God hid him in the back of a desert where no one could see him; many years later, He lifted him up and crowned him king of Israel. Everyone saw him then.

It's easy to fall into the trap of thinking that God chooses people who have it all together. In reality, the Bible teaches the exact opposite: it appears that God chooses foolish and weak things of the world.

**1 Corinthians 1:27 But God has chosen the foolish things of the world to put to shame the wise, and God has chosen the weak things of the world to put to shame the things which are mighty;**

God chooses imperfect and improbable people. For example, Moses was a murderer, Abraham at times was weak and afraid, and Saul of Tarsus persecuted and killed Christians. Yet God chose them anyway.

David was not born with a silver spoon in his mouth. By worldly standards, he was an unlikely candidate to be used by God. When God sent the prophet Samuel to anoint a new king for Israel, David was in the desert watching sheep and goats.[57] He was the youngest son and his father did not have

---

57) 1 Samuel 16:11 Then Samuel asked, "Are these all the sons you have?" "There is still the youngest," Jesse replied. "But he's out in the fields watching the sheep and goats."

great plans for his life. Jesse never even imagined his son David as the future king of Israel. His father and his older brothers did not believe in David, King Saul did not believe in him and even Goliath made fun of him. But God believed in him.

The LORD was David's light. God shined His light on the dysfunction of David's life and chose him for His purposes. And as we saw in Chapter 5, when God shines His light on someone, everything changes. Even though we may not have had the same advantages that others had, or we may not have the same resources that others have, He chooses us and shines His light on us. Even though some people around us may not have believed in us and may even have opposed us, God still has a plan for us and continues to shine His light on us.

Some are lifted up because they push themselves, others because they step on people, others still because they have connections and know the "right" people. In reality, we don't need to manipulate anyone or anything, because the Lord wants to lift us up. In fact, David calls Him the lifter of our heads:

**Psalms 3:3 But You, O Lord, are a shield for me, My glory and the One who lifts up my head.**

God is the one who lifts us up! Like King David, we can be living in obscurity in the back of the desert, and God can take us and thrust us under His spotlight.

The apostle James re-affirms this truth in his epistle:

**James 4:6 But He gives more grace. Therefore He says: "God resists the proud, But gives grace to the humble."**

When He chooses us, we don't have try to make a name for ourselves, print new business cards, open a new website and Facebook page. We don't need to hang out with the right people in the right circles. We don't even need to be jealous of anyone or be intimidated by anybody. And we definitely don't need to step on others or harm them in order to get ahead. Since He resists the proud, all these carnal efforts will be met with opposition by God. We don't want God to resist us; rather, we want His grace to lift us. God does not want us to promote ourselves, He wants to do it.

James continues to explain the best way to get results:

**James 4:10 Humble yourselves in the sight of the Lord, and He will lift you up.**

God does not want us to stay low, He wants to promote us. Our part is to humble ourselves, God's part is to exalt us. Let God do the heavy lifting. Don't promote yourself, let Him promote you.

Many wonder how long this will take. When will God lift me up? I will give you the exact time of your exaltation. The apostle Peter is very precise on the matter of timing:

**1 Peter 5:6 Therefore humble yourselves under the mighty hand of God, that He may exalt you in due time,**

God will exalt you *in due time*. He will do it in *His* time. He will do it at the *right* time. You concentrate on humbling yourself and obeying Him, and He takes care of promoting you. Simple, isn't it?

In the sixth verse of our text David explains:

**Psalms 27:6 And now my head shall be lifted up above my enemies all around me; Therefore I will offer sacrifices of joy in His tabernacle; I will sing, yes, I will sing praises to the Lord.**

David offered sacrifices of joy and sang praises to the Lord, and God lifted him up above his enemies. Lift up your arms and hands to God in praise,[58] and He will lift you up above your troubles.

*The Lord is my light, my salvation and my fortress; therefore, I will not fear. No one and no circumstance can hurt me! He lifts my head above trouble.*

---

58) Wherefore lift up the hands which hang down... (KJV)

# Chapter 9
# Which temple?

## Anyone welcome any time

The time has now come to answer the question we posed at the beginning of the previous chapter: what house and what temple was David referring to?

Let's start by looking again at the fourth verse:

**Psalms 27:4 One thing I have desired of the Lord, That will I seek: That I may dwell in the house of the Lord All the days of my life, To behold the beauty of the Lord, And to inquire in His temple.**

King David expresses a strong desire to dwell in the house of the Lord. What house is he talking about? He also wants to inquire in His temple. Again: what temple is David talking about?

We know that Solomon, David's son, built God a great temple. It was magnificent, and it was one of the wonders of the ancient world. However, it's important to note that when David wrote this Psalm, the temple had not yet been built. Therefore, when David talks about dwelling in the house of the Lord and inquiring in His temple, he could not have been talking about Solomon's temple. This is a surprising affirmation, because it would seem natural to associate David's phrase with the first temple.

When David states that he desires to dwell in the house of the LORD all the days of his life, he does not mean that he wants to stay in the temple twenty-four hours a day. This would not be possible for two reasons: first because, as we just stated, it had not yet been built and second because it would not be physically possible. One cannot stay in a temple, or a church, twenty-four hours a day.

So, what did David mean? The Word Biblical Commentary sheds some light on this question. It states that David is expressing a desire to live every day of his life in the presence of God.[59] He wants to live in constant communion with the LORD.

David goes on to say that he desires to behold the beauty of the LORD. The Amplified version puts it this way:

**Psalm 27:4 ...to behold and gaze upon the beauty [the sweet attractiveness and the delightful loveliness] of the Lord (AMP)**

"Beauty", "sweet attractiveness" and "delightful loveliness" are all terms that imply enjoyment. We enjoy looking at a beautiful painting or a beautiful sunset, and husbands who are happily married enjoy spending time with their lovely wives. David is saying that he wants to live his life enjoying the presence of God all day long, every day of his life. He enjoyed spending time contemplating the beauty, sweet attractiveness and delightful loveliness of God's wonderful presence.

---

59) WBC 2012 Edition. (Jun 15, 2016, 21:07:43 PDT). *Word Biblical Commentary (60 Vols)*. Thomas Nelson.

David concludes the verse by stating that he wants to inquire in His temple. Webster's dictionary definition of "inquire" is "to ask about, to seek information by questioning, to make investigation or inquiry".[60] In other words, David wants to ask God questions about his life and seek information about the situations he was facing. This is why the WBC commentary states that "inquiring in His temple" has to do with seeking divine guidance.[61] David wanted to know God's will for His life. There was continuous dialogue between God and David: David inquired of God, and God answered David and told him what to do.

In short, David expressed a burning desire to be in constant communion with God, enjoying His presence and seeking divine guidance for his life. Is it any wonder that the Bible states that David was a man after God's own heart?

**Acts 13:22 ...He raised up for them David as king, to whom also He gave testimony and said, "I have found David the son of Jesse, a man after My own heart, who will do all My will.'**

All of us should desire the exact same thing: our hearts should seek God, and we should desire to do His will in our lives. The apostle Paul said:

**Romans 8:14 For as many as are led by the Spirit of God, these are sons of God. (NKJ version)**

Those who follow God are led by the Spirit of God. Before choosing a mate or choosing a career we should inquire what His will is. Similarly, before entering into a

---

60) Merriam-Webster. (2008). *Merriam-Webster's 11th Collegiate Dictionary.* Fogware Publishing, Art Software Inc. and Data Storage Research LLC.
61) WBC 2012 Edition.

business deal, we should ask God if it is His will for us. Likewise, we should buy the home God wants us to buy, and attend the church He tells us to attend. Before doing anything, we should ask the Lord what His will is.

Note the words in our text that have been underlined:

**Psalms 27:4 One thing I have desired of the Lord, That will I seek: That I may dwell in the _house_ of the Lord All the days of my life, To behold the beauty of the Lord, And to inquire in His _temple_.**

**Psalms 27:5 For he will conceal me there when troubles come; he will hide me in his _sanctuary_. He will place me out of reach on a high rock.**

David is referring to the "house" of the Lord, also called "temple" or "sanctuary", yet it had not been built. It's true that the tabernacle of Moses was still in existence, but it was not in Israel at this time. So, what exactly is David saying?

We have now come to possibly the main reason why King David was in a class all his own. It seems that David was already experiencing the reality of a sanctuary separate and distinct from the tabernacle of Moses and the temple of Solomon.

James, at the Jerusalem Council, explains:

**Acts 15:16 'After this I will return And will rebuild the tabernacle of David, which has fallen down; I will rebuild its ruins, And I will set it up;**

Notice that the phrase used is "tabernacle of David", *not*

tabernacle of Moses, nor temple of Solomon. *Tabernacle of David.* Simply put, the tabernacle of David was an invisible one, it was the one he built by praising God and living in His presence.

Note how James continues his speech:

**Acts 15:17 So that the rest of mankind may seek the Lord, Even all the Gentiles who are called by My name, Says the Lord who does all these things.'**

*So that the rest of mankind may seek the Lord.* It all has to do with the presence of God, with seeking His face. Spiritually speaking, David was way ahead of his time: he was already living in the presence of God without going to any physical temple.

The Bible is all about the presence of God. It always has been. In the beginning, God planted in the earth the Garden of Eden, a very special place where His presence resided. It was there that God met with man.[62] Many years later, God told Moses to build a tabernacle, and His presence lived there. Finally, He told Solomon to build a temple, and that is where He dwelt. But all these things were temporary, because there would come a time when God would no longer live in temples made by the hands of man. Paul made this crystal clear in his sermon in the Areopagus in Athens:

**Acts 17:24 "He is the God who made the world and everything in it. Since he is Lord of heaven and earth, he doesn't live in man-made temples,**

---

62) Genesis 3:8 When the cool evening breezes were blowing, the man and his wife heard the Lord God walking about in the garden...

God no longer lives in temples made by man. Where then does He live? He lives in temples of flesh!

**1 Corinthians 3:16 Don't you realize that all of you together are the temple of God and that the Spirit of God lives in you?**

**1 Corinthians 6:19 Don't you realize that your body is the temple of the Holy Spirit, who lives in you and was given to you by God? You do not belong to yourself,**

Every born-again believer is the temple of God. God now lives in tabernacles of flesh: He lives in the hearts of men and women who have received Jesus as Saviour. This was His plan all along!

David was especially enlightened not just because he was consecrated to God, but also because of his views on the temple and the presence of God. He was already grasping the concept of an omnipresent, invisible God, accessible anywhere, anytime to anyone who desires His presence.

It is really important to understand the full implication of the following verse:

**Psalms 22:3 Yet you are holy, enthroned on the praises of Israel.**

God is enthroned on the praises of Israel. David understood that God lives in the midst of the praises of His people. Our praise becomes a throne upon which God can sit. Stated another way, our praise builds God a temple, or a home, in which He can live.

Even the apostle Peter makes a strong connection between temple and praise:

**1 Peter 2:5 you also, as living stones, are being built up a spiritual house, a holy priesthood, to offer up spiritual sacrifices acceptable to God through Jesus Christ.** (NKJV)

**1 Peter 2:9 But you *are* a chosen generation, a royal priesthood, a holy nation, His own special people, that you may proclaim the praises of Him who called you out of darkness into His marvelous light; (NKJV)**

We are God's temple, a spiritual house for God to live in, and we proclaim His praises.

Putting it all together, how does this work? We are the temple of God, and we carry His presence in us wherever we go. We don't need to go on a pilgrimage to a faraway temple in order to find God. He is always inside of us. He lives in our praise.

Our text affirms that while I am in trouble God hides me:

**Psalms 27:5 For he will conceal me there when troubles come; he will hide me in his sanctuary. He will place me out of reach on a high rock.**

So, when I am in danger, and I praise Him, God hides me in His presence. He does this anywhere I am. He does this everywhere I am. He does this no matter what circumstances I find myself in. If I worship God in the midst of danger, evil can't touch me anymore, evil can't find me anymore, because God has hidden me in His safe house.

*The Lord is my light, my salvation and my fortress; therefore, I will not fear. No one and no circumstance can hurt me! He lifts my head above trouble. I will live in His Presence all day long.*

# Chapter 10
# The secret

### Walking with God every single day

We are fast approaching the end of our meditation. As promised in the beginning of this study, we will now look at some of David's greatest secrets to overcoming the many challenges he faced in his life. Actually, we have already seen them in the previous chapters. At this juncture, we will put it all together and try to spell out the essence of his tremendous walk with God and success in life.

We will begin by turning our attention to the first part of verse 4:

**Psalms 27:4 One thing I have desired of the Lord, That will I seek: That I may dwell in the house of the Lord All the days of my life, To behold the beauty of the Lord, And to inquire in His temple.**

One thing I have desired of the Lord. *One thing.*

Let's digress for one minute. David desired one thing. How many things are we desiring? Maybe we desire a new car, a better house, a more elegant suit, or a job that pays more. Let there be no misunderstanding: these are all legitimate desires. Jesus did not say that we can't ask God for things. Quite the opposite. He made this very clear in His Sermon on the Mount:

**Matthew 7:7 "Keep on asking, and you will receive what you ask for. Keep on seeking, and you will find. Keep on knocking, and the door will be opened to you.**

Our Lord Himself encouraged us to ask God for things. And He is so good that in the next verse He reveals to us the Father's willingness to grant our requests:

**Matthew 7:8 For everyone who asks, receives. Everyone who seeks, finds. And to everyone who knocks, the door will be opened.**

It is right to ask God for things, and when we do ask Him for something, we can expect to receive it from Him.

Jesus said something really important earlier in the same sermon, something that also has to do with what our priorities should be:

**Matthew 6:33 But seek first the kingdom of God and His righteousness, and all these things shall be added to you.**

Focus. Seek first the kingdom of God. David said "one thing", Jesus said "seek first". Both are telling us to concentrate and keep our priorities straight. And the text reassures us that we don't have to worry about material things, because they will be added to us.

In reality, the Bible does not instruct us to chase after things. We are supposed to chase God, and in turn things chase us. This is exactly what Moses said in the book of Deuteronomy:

**Deuteronomy 28:1-2 "Now it shall come to pass, if you diligently obey the voice of the Lord your God, to observe carefully all His commandments which I command you today, that the Lord your God will set you high above all nations of the earth. ² And all these blessings shall come upon you and overtake you, because you obey the voice of the Lord your God..."**

We seek God, we do our best to please Him and obey Him, and all kinds of blessings will come upon us and overtake us. Just like in a football game one player chases another and tackles him to the ground, so blessings chase us and tackle us to the ground. Life, lived the way God wants us to live it, is fun!

Based on what Jesus and Moses said in the above Scriptures, we don't have to worry about material things. God will add them to us; no worries on that front.

This last sentence is the reason why we digressed concerning this aspect of "one thing". We should not fall in the trap of thinking that we can only seek that one thing and nothing else. That couldn't be the real meaning because Jesus said seek "first" the kingdom of God. The term *first* implies that there is a second, a third, a fourth, etc. It's talking about a priority: first we seek the kingdom, then everything else. First we seek God's presence, then a wife, and a house, and a job, and a car, and clothes, and friends, and recreation, and so on and so forth.

In our text David is saying something else, much broader in scope and higher in importance. He is saying that in the difficult moments of life, when fear, hurtful people and adverse circumstances have declared war on us, we need to concentrate primarily on this one thing: staying in the presence of God.

Each Psalms gives us valuable insights into David's thought process. Psalms 27 in particular shows us that David was an extremely focused individual. The WBC says that this phrase has no parallels among the biblical numerical sayings; it is one of the "most single-minded statements of purpose to be found anywhere in the Old Testament."[63] When inward fears, other people and adverse circumstances all tried to pull him away from God, he did not permit it. He simply did not allow anything to separate him from God's presence. No distractions allowed. No taking our eyes off the Lord.

We must think like David thought. We will keep on seeking His presence even in the midst of the most difficult circumstances. The enemy may at times turn up the heat in the furnace of life to cause a rift between God and us: we must be as determined as David was to not let that happen.

When the pressure is on, we must resist the temptation to complain and fall away from God. Unfortunately, there are those who quit when the going gets tough. They pray to God, the answer does not seem to come as quickly as they would like, so they stop serving Him. They go to the doctor, receive bad news, ask "why me, God?" and stop believing. Or they decide they want to be more generous, they start giving more offerings, the enemy attacks their finances, money becomes tight, and so they stop giving to the church. But, thank God, there are also many of us who don't quit and keep on going no matter what life throws our way.

In Chapter 6, we saw that in this earthly life we will always face challenges. Since there will probably never be a time when we will be completely problem free, then it becomes paramount to learn how to react to problems.

---

63) WBC 2012 Edition. (Jun 15, 2016, 21:07:43 PDT). *Word Biblical Commentary (60 Vols)*. Thomas Nelson.

It is important to realize that it's not the problems per se that cause us to quit, but it's how we react to them that makes the difference between victory and failure. The key is learning how how to think, speak and act in difficult times. In other words, the victory lies in learning how to react to problems.

How do we react? By staying in the presence of God. We learn how to find His presence during difficult times. This was one of the great secrets of David's success in life. He said it himself. In times of trouble, he retreated to his secret place:

**Psalms 27:5 For in the time of trouble He shall hide me in His pavilion; In the secret place of His tabernacle He shall hide me; He shall set me high upon a rock. (NKJV)**

The secret place is like having a getaway hidden high in the mountains or somewhere on an exotic beach. When you are there, no one can find you. The wonderful thing is that it does not take a long time to reach the secret place. Getting there is not complicated, no maps or GPS are needed. It does not require a long and treacherous journey. It is not expensive. The secret place even eliminates the need to go on a religious pilgrimage to a man-made sanctuary in a far-away country.

The terms the Bible uses are clear and indicative of its nature. It is called a "pavilion". According to Webster's dictionary, a pavilion is "a large sumptuous *tent*." It is also called a "tabernacle". Both Moses and David used this term. Webster's dictionary defines tabernacle as a "*tent* sanctuary." In other words, the secret place is a *tent*.

This means that the secret place is portable; we take it with us wherever we go. Like a camping tent, we can erect it and seek refuge in it any time we want to.

Let's break it down even more. Where *exactly* is this secret place and how to we enter?

We have already seen that the secret place is wherever we are. The only thing that remains to be seen is how we enter. It just so happens that the door of entrance is praise:

**Psalms 100:4 Enter his gates with thanksgiving; go into his courts with praise. Give thanks to him and praise his name.**

Like David, we enter the secret place of God's presence by praising Him. When we praise Him, His presence surrounds us and erects a tent of protection around us. Once we are in, we worship Him, we seek His face, and enjoy His presence.

We keep ourselves in His presence by rejoicing:

**Nehemiah 8:10 And Nehemiah continued, "Go and celebrate with a feast of rich foods and sweet drinks, and share gifts of food with people who have nothing prepared. This is a sacred day before our Lord. Don't be dejected and sad, for the joy of the Lord is your strength!"**

The joy of the Lord is our strength. Joy keeps us in the secret place and gives us the strength to persevere in difficult times.

David also mentions joy in our text:

**Psalms 27:6 Then I will hold my head high above my enemies who surround me. At his sanctuary I will offer sacrifices with shouts of joy, singing and praising the Lord with music.**

David said he held his head up high above his enemies, the very enemies he listed in the previous verses. We must hold our heads up high in front of fears, people who want to hurt us and conflicts that seem like wars. Not only do we hold our heads up high, we shout for joy, sing and praise God. Indeed, we count it all joy, just like James said.[64]

One of the most important lessons we must learn in life is to rejoice in times of trouble. As we saw in Chapter 7, we don't rejoice because we like to suffer. We don't even rejoice because we ignore reality and refuse to face the facts. We are not crazy. We rejoice in difficult times because we know the end intended by the Lord. We know that when we come out on the other side we will be better off than when the trouble started. We are sure that God will rescue us.

David was totally convinced of this reality:

**Psalms 56:11 I trust in God, so why should I be afraid? What can mere mortals do to me?**

I trust in God, why should I be afraid? What can mere mortals do to me? David was thoroughly convinced that no ill-intentioned person and no adverse circumstance could harm him.

---

64) James 1:2 Dear brothers and sisters, when troubles come your way, consider it an opportunity for great joy.

Let's go back to the secret place and see what other characteristics is has. David also refers to it in Psalm 91:

**Psalms 91:1 He who dwells in the secret place of the Most High Shall abide under the shadow of the Almighty. (NKJV)**

In the secret place, we abide under the shadow of the Almighty. In other words, we are in the presence of Almighty God. The secret place where David hid was the presence of God.

The secret place is a place of protection:

**Psalms 91:2 This I declare about the Lord: He alone is my refuge, my place of safety; he is my God, and I trust him.**

"Fortress, refuge, safety" – these are words that David used often. They denote the fact that the secret place is secure; when we are in it, no one can find us and nothing can touch us.

In the secret place, there is no fear:

**Psalms 91:5 Do not be afraid of the terrors of the night, nor the arrow that flies in the day.**

In the secret place, there is victory:

**Psalms 91:9-13 If you make the Lord your refuge, if you make the Most High your shelter, [10] no evil will conquer you; no plague will come near your home. [11] For he will order his angels to protect you wherever you go. [12] They will hold you up with their hands so you won't even hurt your foot on a stone. [13] You will trample upon lions and cobras; you will crush fierce lions and serpents under your feet!**

When we take refuge in the secret place, no evil and no plague can come near us, God orders his angels to protect us, and we crush problems under our feet. There is no demon, hurtful person or adverse circumstance that can separate us from God's wonderful presence.

Paul and David were very similar in their way of thinking. The Great Apostle had the same over-the-top faith and confidence in God that the Great King had. Look at what he wrote:

**Romans 8:31 What shall we say about such wonderful things as these? If God is for us, who can ever be against us?**

Nobody can be against us, if God is for us. He then continues by making a long list of things that cannot ever separate us from God:

**Romans 8:35 Can anything ever separate us from Christ's love? Does it mean he no longer loves us if we have trouble or calamity, or are persecuted, or hungry, or destitute, or in danger, or threatened with death?**

**Romans 8:38-39 And I am convinced that nothing can ever separate us from God's love. Neither death nor life, neither angels nor demons, neither our fears for today nor our worries about tomorrow—not even the powers of hell can separate us from God's love. [39] No power in the sky above or in the earth below—indeed, nothing in all creation will ever be able to separate us from the love of God that is revealed in Christ Jesus our Lord.**

The list is pretty exhaustive! And none of these things can separate us from the presence of God.

The next statement made by Paul exudes great confidence:

**Romans 8:37 No, despite all these things, overwhelming victory is ours through Christ, who loved us.**

Not just victory, but *overwhelming* victory. In Christ, we don't just win, we triumph! What a sure, bold, confident, outrageous, over-the-top declaration of faith.

I am convinced that it was the Bible, not modern-day motivational authors, that invented positive thinking. For instance, look at how positive the apostle Paul was:

**Philippians 4:8 And now, dear brothers and sisters, one final thing. Fix your thoughts on what is true, and honorable, and right, and pure, and lovely, and admirable. Think about things that are excellent and worthy of praise.**

Think about things that true, honorable, right, pure, lovely, admirable, excellent and worthy of praise. It doesn't get any more positive than this, does it? Unfortunately, this list excludes most of what we see on television today. Diving into the Word of God is much more constructive than watching television.

This book is not based on the power of positive thinking; it is based on the power of Bible-thinking. It is good to think positive. The Bible encourages it, and Bible-thinking happens to be positive. But positive thinking alone can only get us so far in life. We will eventually face situations which positive thinking alone will not be able to fix. It will take the supernatural power of God to overcome.

Here an example of the power of Bible-thinking from our text:

**Psalms 27:3 Though an army may encamp against me, My heart shall not fear; Though war may rise against me, In this I will be confident.**

David is *extremely* positive. The *New King James* version of the Bible gives a title to every Psalm. The title it gives this Psalm is *"An Exuberant Declaration of Faith."* In the same vein, Walvoord and Zuck entitle it *"Confidence that dispels fear"*, and characterize it as a Psalm of courageous trust.[65] In other words, David is expressing unwavering confidence, uplifting hope and outrageous joy in the midst of all kinds of dangers. I will not fear, I will trust God, I will be confident, I will rejoice – *take that, devil*!

Some may object and think that we are being arrogant. Don't worry, this is not arrogance. This is Bible-based boldness. Not only is it right, the Scripture actually encourages it.

Remember, the Lord is your light:

**Psalms 27:1 The Lord is my light and my salvation—so why should I be afraid? The Lord is my fortress, protecting me from danger, so why should I tremble?**

Our confidence is not based on our intelligence, bravery or strength. Our boldness is not based on our abilities or

---

65) Walvoord, J. F. & Zuck, R. B. (1985). *The Bible Knowledge Commentary: An Exposition of the Scriptures (2 Vols)*. Wheaton, IL: Victor Books.

talents. We are not that special. Our confidence is firmly based on God's willingness and ability to rescue us. He is our strength, we are not afraid because the Lord is our light and our salvation. He is our light, and we are *fearless in the light*.

*The Lord is my light, my salvation and my fortress; therefore, I will not fear. No one and no circumstance can hurt me! He lifts my head above trouble. I will live in His Presence all day long, and I will not let anything separate me from the presence of God.*

*I am fearless in the light and fearless in all circumstances!*

# APPENDIX
# *Pantophobia no more*

## *Delivered from all my phobias*

In Chapter 5, we studied the following verse:

**Psalms 34:4 I prayed to the Lord, and he answered me. He freed me from all my fears.**

According to psychologists, there are more than 300 phobias. Here are some of them:

| | |
|---|---|
| Acrophobia: | fear of heights |
| Claustrophobia: | fear of confined spaces |
| Agoraphobia: | fear of open places |
| Gephyrophobia: | fear of bridges |
| Anthrophobia: | fear of humans |
| Cynophobia: | fear of dogs |
| Kleptophobia: | fear of theft |
| Aquaphobia: | fear of water |
| Brontophobia: | fear of thunder and lightning |
| Dentophobia: | fear of dentists |
| Sciophobia: | fear of shadows |
| Cardiophobia: | fear of heart disease |
| Triskaidekaphobia: | fear of the number 13 |
| Amaxophobia: | fear of riding in a vehicle |
| Anuptaphobia: | fear of remaining unmarried |
| Hematophobia: | fear of seeing blood |
| Peniaphobia: | fear of poverty |
| Tropophobia: | fear of changing |
| Thanatophobia: | fear of death |
| Pantophobia: | fear of everything |

Thank God He delivered us from *all* our fears!

# *The Most Important Decision in Life*

Dear friend,

If you don't have a dynamic, exciting relationship with God, then now is the time to do something about it.

Maybe you are a "good" person, one who has always lived right; thank God for this. Or maybe you have made some bad choices, and your life is a mess. Either way, we all need God's unmerited favour in our lives. We are not saved by our good behaviour: we are saved by God's grace.

In order to be absolutely sure that your sins are forgiven, that you have eternal life, and that you will spend all of eternity in heaven with God, we invite you to pray this short prayer:

*"Heavenly Father, I come to you in the Name of Jesus. I give you my life. I believe that Jesus died and rose again for me. Jesus, I invite you to come into my heart. Please forgive all my sins, and make me a brand-new person. I will follow You and serve You all the days of my life. I pray in the Name of Jesus, Amen."*

Congratulations! If your prayer was sincere, you are now born-again. You are a new person in Christ. The Bible states that the past has been erased and everything in your life has become new:

**2 Corinthians 5:17 This means that anyone who belongs to Christ has become a new person. The old life is gone; a new life has begun!**

This is a fresh start. However, it is only the first step. We would like to help you by sending you material which will show you what the next steps are in your new exciting walk with God. The material we will send you is 100% free and there is absolutely no obligation of any kind. Here is our contact information:

info@goodnewsint.org

We really look forward to hearing from you.

Thank you, and may God's rich, abundant blessings always be in your life.

# *About Good News Ministries*

Max and Connie Girgenti founded Good News Ministries in 1994. The mission is *transforming nations one person at a time*. This is accomplished by reaching the lost, teaching the believers and training local pastors in various nations of the world.

As of this writing, Max and Connie have planted one church in Canada and four churches in Italy. They direct three Bible Schools whose purpose is to train pastors and leaders in sound biblical principles. They also oversee a network of Italian churches and ministers, which provides continuous training to many pastors and leaders. Furthermore, the ministry organizes national yearly conferences and monthly local meetings in various regions of the nation.

In addition, Good News Ministries has translated and printed over 50 books, which have been instrumental in bringing the Gospel of Jesus Christ to many Italian speaking communities around the world.

Finally, the humanitarian work of the ministry consists of supporting foster homes and orphanages, and sending books free of charge to inmates in several prisons.

For more information, and to see how you can help us fulfill the vision, please visit our website:
http://www.goodnewsint.org

Or contact us at:
info@goodnewsint.org

**Other Products:**

Audio Teaching – Max Girgenti

Be Happy
From Here to There
God Has Given You Dreams
Kick Like Heck
Living the Life of Faith
Run to Win
Tests, Trials, Temptations
The WOW Factor of Jesus
What to do in Difficult Times

Preparing For Your Future
Taking Back
From the Pit to the Palace

E-book:
The Beauty of Holiness

For complete lists of products:
www.goodnewsint.org